SECRET TO SELL MORE THAN 100 EBOOKS IN FIRST 4 DAYS

By -- Max

YouTube Channel :

https://www.youtube.com/channel/UC17jVFBVBhQWv1FRqd8Yidg

Blog : www.seriousearning.blogspot.pt

You can earn a lot more than the price of this book from this particular eBook. I have just put some price because if you pay for something even if it is small penny you **take it seriously and try to gain something from it**. I assure you if you do things as described in this book and put your sincere efforts you can earn even thousands of dollars depending on your dedication. I am no different than you, if I can sell more than 100 books in less than 4 days, I am sure **you can sell a lot more** than that.

This is the first book of the series in which I would be telling *all the different and easy ways you can make money online sitting at home for free and very effectively without investing even a single penny* . This is not the book that I am doing just for the name sake, when I am saying it I can help you in making some money, I really mean by it. I am man of my words.

Hello guys, let me introduce myself. Well, my name is MAX and I am going to show you the way on how to write an eBook from scratch even if you don't know anything about computers and internet. It just needs a computer or a laptop and internet connection and anybody can get benefit from this, be it young students looking for extra money, moms that are having some time to spend or our senior citizens, this book is for everybody. Well the biggest benefit is that **you don't need to spend even a single penny from your hard earned money**, You can start literally from scratch just like I did some time back. In this eBook, I am going to disclose all the tricks and path that I followed which led me to *sell more than 100 books just on kindle in the very first 4 days of publishing my book*. I have written a book few days back and that was my first eBook that I wrote myself and published on kindle. I did a lot of research before publishing on kindle because I was completely new to this platform, I didn't knew how to write an eBook, where to publish, how to make some money (that works as motivation to write more). I didn't have any idea about all this. I also bought some products but most of that was crap and I was not able to get any benefit from that. After researching for a lot of time, I finally decided to write an eBook and all the techniques I learned from my research, I implemented in it. I was very surprised on observing the results, the book sold more than 100 times just on kindle in just 4 days and I was very happy with my progress. I was also able to make good amount of money from it. Now, I want to help you out in writing an eBook and market it so that you can also get benefit from it and make some money if you like (That I think everybody likes) from the comfort of your home and spend your free time into some productive work. You could do this on Sundays or in the night or whenever you are having time.

-- I have given links in this eBook from where you can get the public domain eBooks for free and republish it in your name to get money but you have to find it in this eBook where are the links . . . now the only thing that is prohibiting you from making money for free are just those links, If you have guts find it and get money . . . as simple as that . . .

In this book basically I will show or tell you about --

- *How to write a book from scratch even if you don't have any knowledge about writing books.*
- *How to make money even if you don't want to write your own eBook.*
- *What are public domain books and private domain books.*
- *How to select a hot subject of your interest to sell.*
- *How to do market research and study whether there is a demand for that subject or not.*
- *What are keywords and how they are crucial in determining your success.*
- *Formatting your eBook for kindle devices.*
- *How to sell on kindle and other platforms or publishing your eBook to different platforms.*
- *How to publish the physical hard copy of your book without spending even a single penny.*
- *Different ways of promoting your books to sell more.*
- *Marketing your eBooks on different platforms online Social media promotion.*
- *Useful tips.*

In this book I have used data all written by myself and literally based on my experiences. I would be covering the steps important for publishing a successful eBook on kindle. Although there are many other platforms that you can use to sell your eBooks which also I would be discussing in this book. In this particular eBook you will get answers to following questions :

How can I write a book ?

Why I should write a book ?

What is the benefit of writing an eBook ?

Do I have to spend money also ?

Is the income is just for one time or it is regular ?

How much time I have to spend ?

Is it any fixed time of day that I have to work ?

Can I do this stuff in weekends and still make some cash ?

I don't have a vast knowledge on any particular topic so, how can I write a book on that ?

. . . . .

The list of questions is very large and all the answers you are going to find here in this just one eBook.

This is just investment for making money and what could be better than investing as little as a cup of coffee for all the assets that you are going to get in just one book in the form of knowledge and we all have read that "Knowledge is the only thing that cannot be stolen"

So, it would not be wrong to say that you are getting an asset that will make you money for the rest of your life and the cost you have to pay is just equal to a cup of coffee.

LET'S START TO WHAT IT IS MEANT FOR . . .

CHAPTER -- 1

How to write a book from scratch even if you don't have any knowledge about writing books.

Writing a book could be very simple no matter if you have the knowledge of that particular subject or not. Although it is an interesting thing if you do it yourself for those who consider books boring, once you start writing it yourself I am sure you would get keen interest in it.

I am going to discuss below some of the answers that I got when I asked people to write a book if they want to get some extra cash per month deposited directly to their bank accounts. The answers were like --

- Oh, I don't know how to write a book. -- *Nobody is born with the knowledge to do any kind of specific job or work, you have to learn.*
- I am not a book worm. -- *There is always a term related bad to every professional, just don't care . . .*
- Oh, It is not in my KARMA -- *If you think like this nothing is in your KARMA, you cannot do anything.*
- Cut the crap it is not easy to write a book. -- *Nothing is easy and nothing is difficult, it is just the way you think it. If you really want it nothing is out of reach of man, every thing is easy.*
- I cant sit back and write so many pages -- *It does not need to continuously sit back and keep on writing till the book ends. You can write 1-2 pages every time you are free.*
- I am not SHAKESPEARE -- *Yeah, even SHAKESPEARE was not "THE SHAKESPEARE" before he started writing. He was not born with the name you idiot . . .*

So, if you have got any of these reasons, I have got an answer for you . . .

Now, how to write a book, well first of all we all know internet is a huge source of information. You can get any kind of information on any kind of subject and in lots of quantity. Its just the matter of fact about the kind of information or micro subject that you want to provide in your eBook. You have to be very subjective and targeted towards the knowledge you are providing. The major problem is the content, and the solution to that is internet so *the major problem is solved*. Do your homework in a very proper way to select the information to provide in your book because all the information on the internet is even not exactly correct. Research on the subject before writing.

OK, so I can copy and paste the content and just make a book in an hour or two -- *No, select the right content and do your homework before writing any thing. Select the things you would like to read and spend money on because if you are not having any confidence in your stuff then how will other person will feel good to buy it.*

Choose a particular topic and the strategy to find a profitable topic or niche, I have discussed in the later chapter on How to select a hot subject of your interest to sell. Read articles related to that topic, if it is something that you want from your audience to do, first try it yourself and give its reviews or things that worked for you and things that does not worked for you. For example you can talk about some recipes that you tried and you liked it very much. In my case I am doing the thing like how was I able to sell more than hundred copies of my book in four days that I have already done.

There are also **some ways in which you can earn without even writing books by yourself**. These methods have been **discussed in the next chapter**.

CHAPTER - 2

How to make money even if you don't want to write your own eBook.

This chapter would be very important for many people who really want to get some cash by selling eBooks or those who are having a desire to be a writer but due to any reason they could not write by themselves. I did a lot of research on how you can make money by not writing an eBook and only following four ways are there that I think have a great potential --

1) **Publishing Public domain eBooks** -- Now, the public domain eBooks are those which you can republish without taking any permission from anybody or buying rights for that book from anybody. You can just get it, edit it according to your will and republish it on the internet to get some money, *Sounds interesting ?* I have **given the link to the websites from where you can get free public domain eBooks** that you can republish in your name to get money instantaneously, but for that you have to do some work . . .

Yeah, where can I find these books, tell me fast . . .

-- *Search it in this eBook, the links are somewhere in this book, you have work to search it. Get links, get money . . .*

2) **Spend 5 dollars and get everything done** -- The another method is for making money without writing eBooks is that hiring somebody that will write your book on the topic you tell him and the content you tell him, make cover for you and do everything you want him to do for you related to the book. I am giving you the link or the name of the site from where you can get the person that will do everything for you in just 5 bucks.

www.fiverr.com

3) **Getting content from social media** -- This is also a very good method and you don't even need to spend 5 bucks to get content from this method. Just go to any social media website Facebook or twitter or both of them. You can make a page of the subject you want to write an eBook. like recipes, so you make a page and invite people to give their recipes and don't forget to add disclaimer that all stuff on that page will become your property and you can use it anywhere. You can start a competition on your page about best recipes and people start posting their recipes on your page and there you have a lot of content for free. Just copy and paste from your page and make a book and sell on kindle, make money.

4) **Secret Treasure** -- If you are not interested in any of the above and you find it not up to your level, this step is the easiest one and as the name suggests, it is a treasure. I am going to tell you a way in which you can get 1200 books, which you can use in your name. Just keep on adding 1 book every week and see your sale in couple of months. Check out the following link.

http://bit.ly/1HxSf7x

CHAPTER - 3

What are public domain books and private domain books.

It is a very important for those who do not want to write any kind of book by themselves but still want to make money publishing eBooks. It is a very small chapter, here I am going to tell you just the difference between public domain books and private domain books.

Public domain books -- These are those books which are not copyright protected that means that you can sell those eBooks again in your own name. The simplest way to make money just grab some public domain book and upload it to kindle in your name and sell to get money -- What could be better than this now . . .

Again I am telling you there are 3 links that have number of books that you can republish and make money, Show your guts, find it . . . yeah I am not going to give you if you do not put efforts, you will only get it if you really want it . . .abuse me no problem, lol . . .

Ok, cut the crap. I'll reveal the suspense. If you want the links where you can get public domain eBooks just send your name and the country you belong to at --

getmethelinks@gmail.com

and you will get the links within 5 minutes on your email.

The are some more ways to get eBooks in a huge quantity just at one place that you can check at the following link.

http://bit.ly/1HxSf7x

Private domain books -- These are the books that are copyright protected and you cannot republish it on any other form to sell it in your own name. If you write an eBook for your self on any topic, it would be your private domain book and anybody else cannot sell it on internet legally.

CHAPTER - 4

How to select a hot subject of your interest to sell.

Selecting a topic could be very crucial and important aspect because if you choose topic that already have so many books in it, it would create difficulty for you to sell. I am not saying it is impossible but it takes a lot of time to get good ranked in the kindle library if too many books are already there in that particular niche. I have shown some ways which are as follows that will help you choosing the right topic and a profitable niche.

Now, lets talk about the resources that can help you to write an eBook easily. I advice you grab a pen and a paper so that you may be able to learn what are the things on which you could write a book. Just read the following points and write the answers of those points on the paper. lets start -

What are your hobbies or what are your interests ?

  -- If you are not aware of your own interests than you can write answers to following questions. It gives you the overview of all the subjects you would feel happy to write about.

   -- *What do you like to do in your free time ?*

   -- *What kind of magazines do you like to read ?*

   -- *What topic you talk about mostly with your friends ?*

   -- *When you go to the supermarket what are things that you spent most of the time searching for ?*

Now that you have noted down your interests and hobbies, search on the internet what amongst your interests and hobbies are the most selling topics and books. Even if there is no topic that you have came up with amongst best selling list you can still publish book in your interest, you just have to watch out similar books to your topic that are best selling and are already there in the kindle and how many of them have sold. Read their description and try to relate it with your eBook like content could be similar but not same. You can also get your eBook ranked just near the best selling eBook, like if people search for that kind of book, the books are shown in selling criteria. For example the best selling would be at the top and then second top selling and so on . . . It is very difficult for your eBook to get in the first page of search but there is a trick with the keywords that you can use to bring your eBook in the first page of the search which I am going to discuss in the later chapter relating to keywords.

There is also one e-book on how to write a best selling e-book. In case if you are a real perfectionist, you may check it . . .

http://bit.ly/1vax04M

One more you can check out is " The e-book university"

http://bit.ly/1B3BQoP

CHAPTER -- 5

How to do market research and study whether there is a demand for that subject or not.

There are some topics which are evergreen like recipes so we can take example of the recipes book, to be more precise we can take Christmas recipes (just because it is Christmas season, at least at the time I am writing this book). This would be an example niche and it is very beneficial for the new comers to select micro niche, I personally suggest that you should **go for micro niche** because --

It gives you more content to write like you can write about different micro niches in the major niche like we have selected recipes as our major niche and sub niche is CHRISTMAS RECIPES and micro niche can be like, lets say CHRISTMAS STARTERS. So, the major benefit of selecting micro niche is that you can write about CHRISTMAS STARTERS and then CHRISTMAS MAIN COURSE and so on . . .

If there is a book on kindle on CHRISTMAS STARTERS, I don't know if it is, If you want you can get it just for case study or go through the page of the book on kindle. You can even lend it for free from kindle select or kindle lending library. It could be your case study about how the book is written and formatted and what kind of content you can write. You can also take it as a case study about how the book is written and formatted.

In my opinion micro niche is important because otherwise every time you have to find new subjects to write about and also your audience also gets scattered, as if you are writing your first book on recipes, you get an image of a chef and if you write your second book on marketing or gadgets or any other stuff, there are very less chances that you survive in the market. So, select your micro niche carefully according to your interest and hobbies.

Now, how to search that there is a demand for the topic you are choosing ?

-- Just go to kindle.amazon.com and search Christmas Starters and you will find no. of books there. You can also check each book's history and reviews like how many of that books have been sold and what is the rank of that book in the kindle store. Less than 10,000 is great because there are millions of books there on each niche and micro niche.

I am doing this for the CHRISTMAS STARTERES as example, you can search for your own niches and interests.

Now, once you find that there are some books so it could be determined that there is some demand. You can also have a look at the no. of books sold. You must see that there should not be so many books because it could raise the competition and make it difficult for you to survive.

Another method of finding that weather people are looking for the topic you are going to write about or not i.e. GOOGLE ADWORDS. It is a very useful tool for the online marketers. There are many paid services that provide this kind of service but google AdWords is completely free and is best for you. Now, here I am going to tell you to use and check that if people are searching for your niche or not. It also tells how much competition is there in your niche. It not only tells the no. of searches that are made on google every month but it can also tell the no. of searches people are making on kindle for your niche. Here I am going to teach you all new tool step by step along with the screen shots.

Firstly you have to have a google account that I am sure you would already be having, If not you can just go to www.gmail.com and sign up for that, it is as simple as that.

Now, go to www.google.com and search for google AdWords then select the first link in the result page, it will take you to another page, just sign in with your google account on that page.

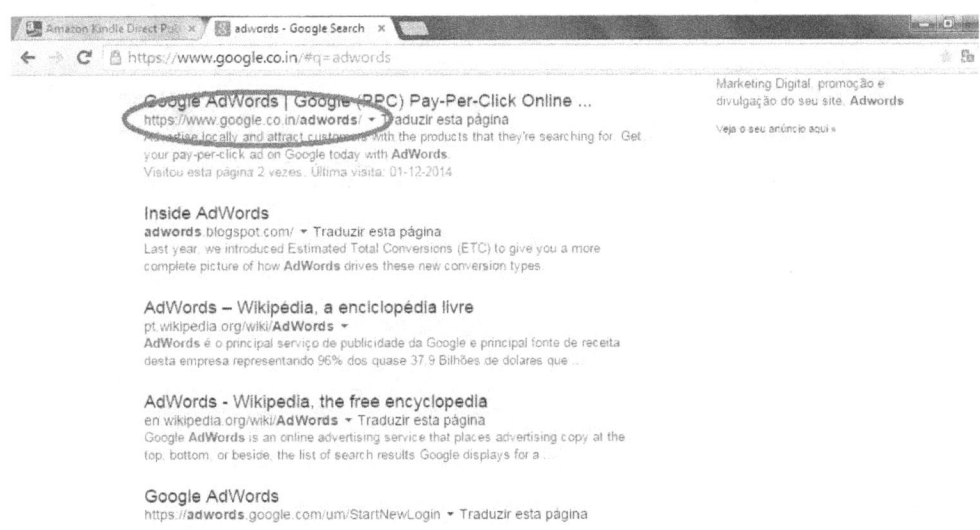

When new page opens then there is an option for sign in with your Gmail account on the top right corner, click there.

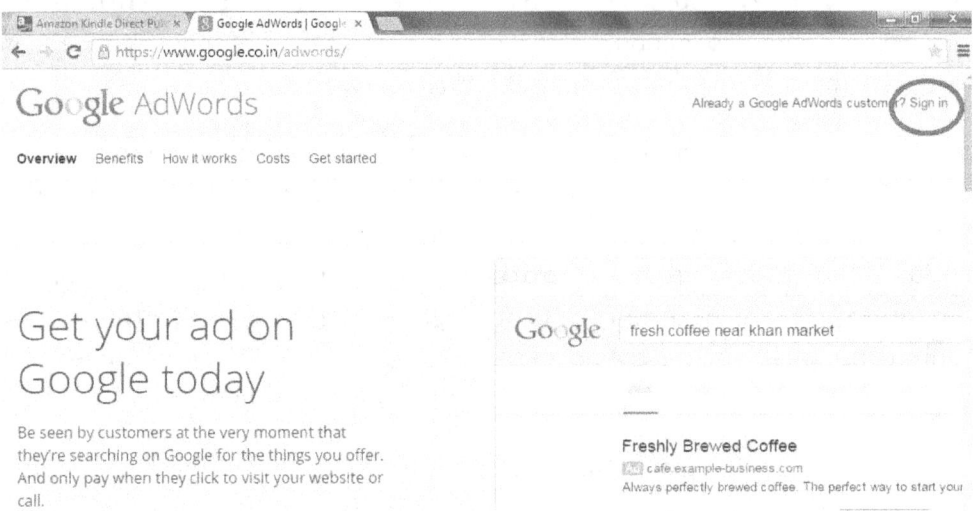

Now, there are many options available but you have to click on "tools" and then "Keyword Planner".

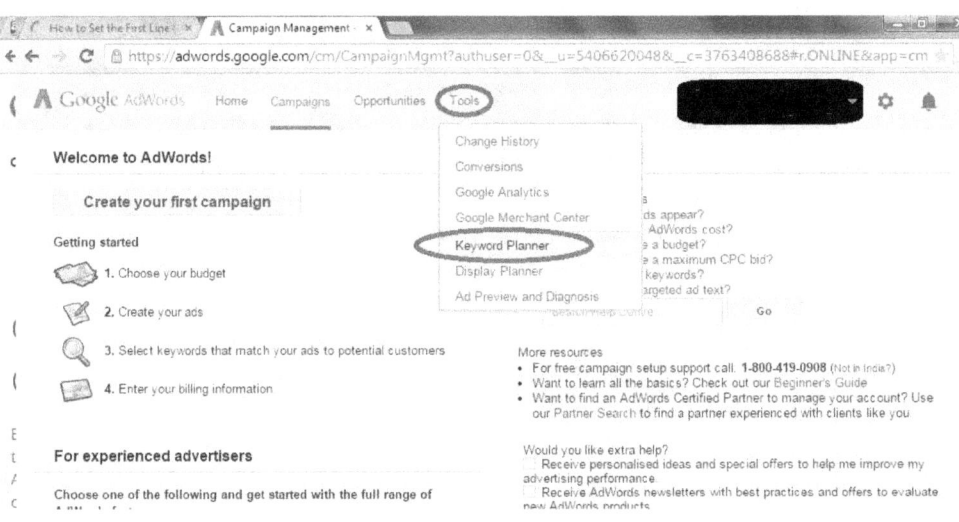

Then it will ask "What you would like to do". Just click on the very first option given that I have encircled it in the screenshot below.

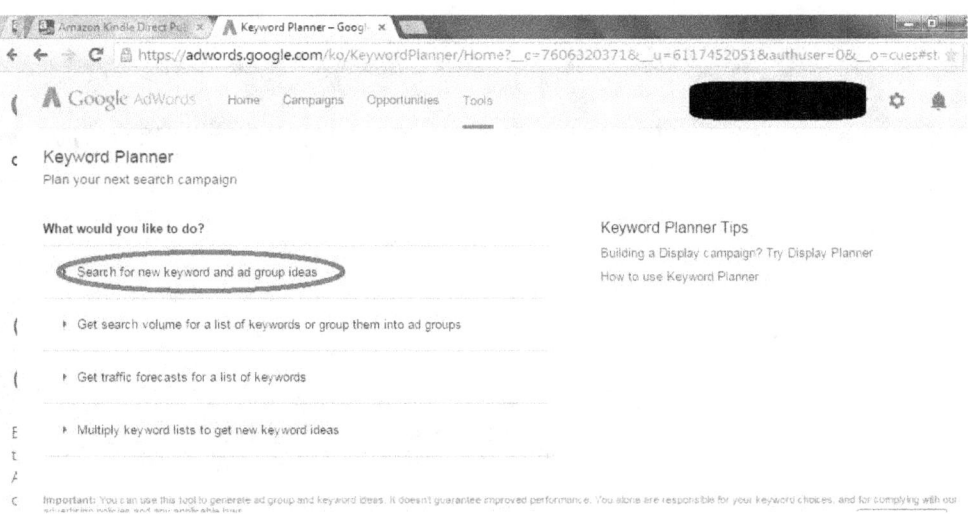

Now, type in your keywords that you want to search for, like I have searched for "Christmas Starters".

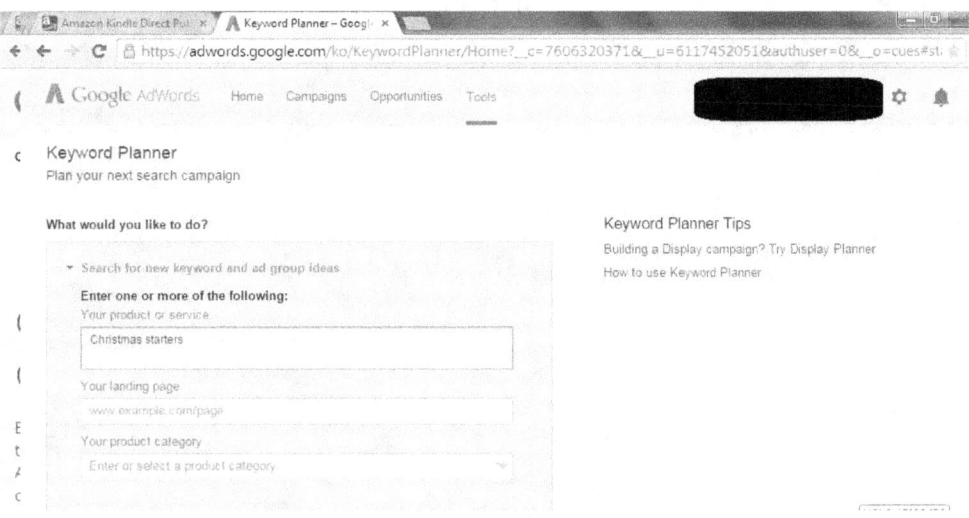

After you are done with your keywords, it will show you the no. of searches being made for that keyword every month. As shown in the screenshot below.

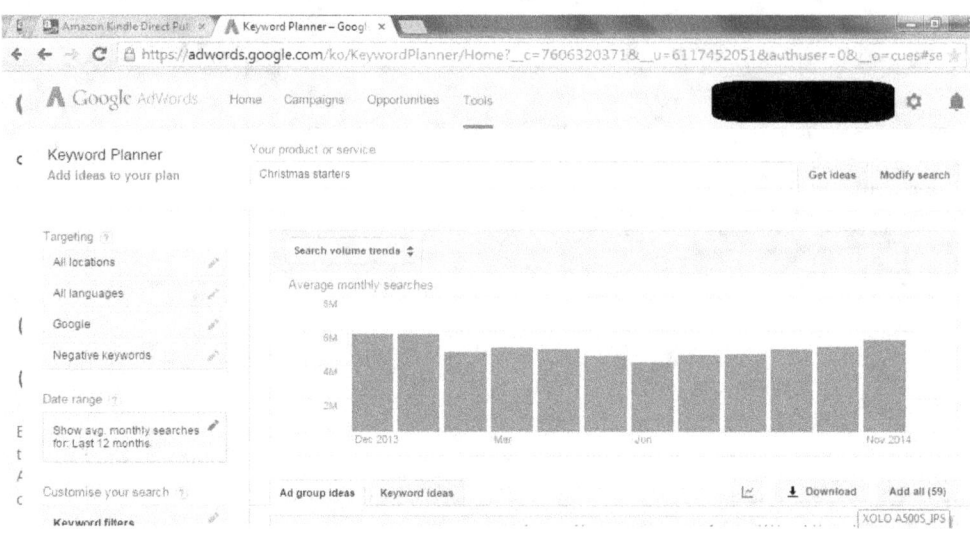

Now, here you can see it shows the result for the last one year and the number of searches that are being made on google every month. Here for the keywords I have entered the no. of searches are anywhere between 4.5 to 6 million. So, that's a good number to start but you also have to check that there should not be too many books already on that.

CHAPTER -- 6

What are keywords and how they are crucial in determining your success.

As I have told in last chapter, keywords are very important factor that has the potential to either boost up your sale or not even letting you start your sale.

Keywords are the words or phrases you type in the search bar of search engine to find something. Just like in google we people type "cars" or "cars with batteries", "how to drive a car", "recipes", "Christmas recipes", 'Christmas starters". These all are keywords and for each keyword you get different results. keywords determine when your book is going to be viewed, like for what keywords should be typed in the search bar that your book should appear. now obviously "CHRISTMAS STARTERS" do not appear when we search for "CARS". I hope you might be having an idea about the keywords.

I know a guy who wrote a book in nine months and uploaded to kindle but he was not even able to sell 1 copy in the first month, he even started a free promotion for his book where he was giving his book for free and still he could not sell even 1 copy that too free. Now, here is what keywords come into play, I am going to tell you the importance of the keywords. When you publish your book on kindle, you are asked to select at least 7- 8 keywords.

As I have told you about google AdWords in previous chapter there you can see no. of searches that are made on "Christmas starters" per month that tells you that there is a demand about that topic. If the number of searches are between 10000-15000, it is enough. Now, you can also see similar keywords relating to your topic for which high searches are being made. Similarly like this you can select at least 7 keywords relating to your book title or content for which the no. of searches being made are high. So, every time people search for those keywords, your book will appear and chances are that your book will be sold.

The another best feature of google AdWords is that you can also see the no. of searches that are made for a particular subject in kindle store also. So, you can see how it can affect your sale. If the no. of searches are more and the no. of books are not too much you can add up to that subject and surely you will get good results.

Now, a simple trick that can rank you amongst top ranking books on search pages is that choose your keywords similar to the best sellers in your subject or niche. You can also choose "best sellers in your topic" as your keyword also. So, when people search for "best sellers in your topic" keywords your book will appear at the top.

This trick nobody will tell you I am sure because this thing is the main thing that is responsible for driving sales. By now, you must have understood about keywords... at least I hope so.

But still, if you have any problem or questions, you can ask your question in the review or comments and I'll be pleased to help you.

CHAPTER -- 7

Formatting your eBook for kindle devices.

This chapter is very simple and it will not even take your much time to read. Actually formatting your book and previewing it are the simplest steps.

Proper formatting of your book is very important because it is going to be read on different platforms like android mobiles and tablets, Apple products and mostly on kindle devices. So, it needs to be properly formatted, so that the text is properly arranged and the pics are placed properly along with the text. Will you read a book if it has unarranged text, lots of spaces between the paragraphs and also some lines going out of form or out of your device screen that you cant even access. So, in order to get a professional looking book you have to properly arrange the text or format the text of your book.

So, how can I do it ??

-- *Don't worry, I am here . . .*

There is a simple tool that is provided by kindle itself and you can download it for free. You can search for kindle formatting tool and you will get a link on google that will take you to its download page and you can download it from there. You can arrange all your text in there easily, you can even preview it and it will show you exactly how it is going to look on the actual device. So, here you can get your book formatted just like professional.

Although there is another tool for preview that also you can download for free and check how your book looks like. So, that was it for this chapter . . . Let's roll onto the next chapter.

CHAPTER -- 8

How to sell on kindle and other platforms or publishing your eBook to different platforms.

Now, here comes the main deal, selling your eBook. Once you have completed your eBook, like writing, editing and formatting. You have made your cover for the book etc. Now, is the time to sell it on kindle and other platforms.

Selling on kindle is easy, I mean the starting process. Like, you just have to make an account on kindle, that you must already be having if you have downloaded from kindle. If you don't have an account. Go to www.kdp.amazon.com and just sign up. "kdp" stands for KINDLE DIRECT PUBLISHING and this is the branch of kindle that allows you to publish your own eBooks. You need to have a bank account in your name so, that you can receive money from amazon. They will ask you to give your TAX id, Bank Account, name of bank, IBAN etc. that if you don't know then you have to contact your bank representative. Once you make an account you can sell unlimited no. of books. Apart from kindle you can also sell your eBook on many other sources.

After you give all your information and start uploading your eBook, the first thing it is going to ask you is that if the book you are uploading is a private domain or public domain. In each case it takes around 12 hours to make your book available at the online store. In case of public domain it will ask you what have you done in the book apart from just copying form one site and trying to upload it on kindle. You have tell if you have added new pictures, edited the text, translated the text or anything that you have done then they will analyze it, if the content is good enough or your contribution is good enough, they will upload it.

What are other sources apart from kindle where I can sell my ebook ?

-- Following is the list of other sources where you can sell your eBook, you just have to create an account and upload your eBook just like you did here on kindle.

- lulu.com
- Barnes and nobles
- Smashwords
- i-book store

Now, these above given are some of the platforms where you can sell your eBooks to get money and by money I mean real passive income.

In this chapter we have covered the different platforms which can be exploited to sell your eBook. Now, how to get sales is another aspect which I will cover in the next chapter. You should not think that just by uploading your book guarantees your regular income, you have to do some marketing, for that I am going to tell you how to do it in the next chapter.

CHAPTER -- 9

How to publish the physical hard copy of your book without spending even a single penny.

If you think that only name of the chapter sounds good, let me tell you I am going t tell you the same thing that I have written as the title of this chapter, no scams or fooling.

Once you have completed your book, uploaded it on various platforms and your book is ready to sale, You can make your book available in physical hard copy form also.

How can I sale physical hard copy without a publishing company ?

Can I really make my book available in physical hard copy form without spending any money ?

The simplest answer to all your questions relating to this chapter is Createspace.

It is a tool from amazon.com that can sale hard copy form of your book. Now, How it works is that once you give the soft copy of your book to them just like kindle, you have to upload it and then if anybody orders the copy of your book from createspace.com, they print the hard copy of your eBook and mail it to the customer's address. You get the money for your book and all the printing, mailing is done by them. You have to worry about nothing, it is truly very simple. Just go to createspace.com and start selling your true hard printed copy of your book.

CHAPTER -- 10

Different ways of promoting your books to sell more.

One of the most important chapters. Ok, now after uploading all your stuff online, making it look nice and selecting keywords etc. The final step comes marketing or promoting. As I have written earlier also, you cannot just upload your book and start thinking that money is going to fall from heaven, NO, its not at all like that you have to do some work, put in your efforts to initialize the sale. Just uploading the book is not enough. Here I am going to tell you about 2 of the kindle inbuilt promoting features under KINDLE SELECT. They are --

1. **KINDLE COUNTDOWN DEALS** -- This is a promotion feature in which you can promote your book at a less price then you have set up. Like, if you have set the price of your book as 5 dollars then you can reduce the price to any amount like 2-3 dollars for certain period of time. This help to grow your sales. By looking onto offers people really get attracted and if you have written something interesting in your description and first page of the book then your book will surely sell. You also get extra income from kindle for doing this like --

If for that month 1 million worth of books have been sold.

and the total no. of books were 3 hundred thousand.

Your book was read more than ten%, 15 hundred times.

So, $15000/300000 = 0.005$

hence, 1 million $*0.005 = 5000$

So, you get an extra 5 thousand dollars just for promoting your book at less price from kindle apart from your royalties.

2. **FREE BOOK PROMOTION** -- In this promotion feature you can give away your book fro free for certain period of time. Here you do not get any extra income from kindle, its just that it adds up to the total books sold till now. The benefit is that there are chances that your rank may rise up if you sell more even for free that increases the chances to get more eyeballs through your eBook leading to more sales.

For me, I used only these two tools and from only these two tools I got more than hundred of my books sold in four days.

So, these are the 2 inbuilt promotion feature of kindle that you can use to get more sales and more cash. There are more methods to promote your book that I am going to discuss with you in the next chapter i.e. social media promotion.

CHAPTER -- 11

Marketing your eBooks on different platforms online Social media promotion.

After utilizing the kindle's in built promotion features, you can use many different platforms to promote your book for free. There are some of the methods that are described as follows --

YouTube -- The greatest ocean of videos on this planet and a great marketing tool. You can make a simple video convincing people to buy your book and the features that you have added to your book. If you are camera conscious you can even make a white board video for your book. if you don't know what a white board video is you can go to google and search it. There is an added benefit of YouTube that not just it is free but you can make money from YouTube also by submitting your videos. You can use google AdSense feature to make money from YouTube also. If you want a deeper knowledge about this, I will be doing book on this also, stay tuned . . .

Facebook -- Another greatest tool for marketing and easy to use. You can just search for pages relating to your topic and post on those pages about your book. Don't write crappy posts like "hey guys, check it out I have got a new book to sell", NO this is totally wrong. Just write simple small article about the topic just like as if you are talking to someone casually and at the last you can write " I have gone through this book, I think it has got some great content, if you are interested, I'll leave a link below " and then you give the link to the page of kindle where your book is published. You can even tell your friends about your book and tell them to share.

Twitter -- You can do the same stuff with twitter also as with the Facebook. Just tweet about your book or you can tweet on the pages relating to your topic. It is also very simple for you and you can do it easily. Again if you have any questions, you can leave in the comments section below of the page from where you got this book.

Use all the social media websites to promote your book. The more you promote, more are the chances of selling your book and greater income you will have.

Blogging -- It is also very effective marketing strategy. You can start your own blog or you can even post on other blogs relating to your subject. Remember always write simple small articles rather than being a salesman trying to sell things by posting creepy lines that no one will even completely read. if you don't know how to find blogs to write onto, you can just go to google and write their your subject like "recipes" and then write "blogs", you will get a huge list of blogs relating to your topic and you can write onto them.

Social forums -- These are also similar to blogs, you can do the same stuff with social forums just like blogs.

Useful tips.

- Never give useless content in your book. Always provide something beneficial and useful to your viewers. Think yourself as a buyer of your book and then write and think if I will give this kind of information will I buy it ? Think as if you are the buyer and always write that things which you feel comfortable spending money on.
- Be Focused, never lose hope, stick with it. Don't expect a high income in the starting, it takes time just like any other business. Keep on working and surely you will get fruitful result.
- Give the information in the new book relevant to your previous book, do not change the main theme. Just I have written before also if you are writing about the recipes, keep on writing about that thing only don't start writing on marketing, farming or automobile engineering etc. This way you will not land anywhere.
- Keep on adding new books to your virtual library.
- Give something convincing in the description and in the first 2-3 pages because that will lead your sale.
- Try to give a good title, because something sets up in the subconscious mind of the people just by looking at the title so, it should not give something negative or opposing.

- For public domain books, read it yourself first before publishing it otherwise you will not succeed. If you read you will know the content of the book and from the response you will get an estimate about what kind of content is selling more so you can provide that kind of books only. You will get to know the taste of your audience.

At last I would like to thank you from deep core of my heart for showing some faith in me. I will keep on writing these methods to make money online without spending even a single penny. My methods would just be requiring your sincere efforts and some time.

HAPPY WRITING

STAY BLESSED STAY HAPPY . . .

Subscribe on to following YouTube channel and blog for more of these methods and video tutorials.

YouTube Channel :

https://www.youtube.com/channel/UC17jVFBVBhQWv1FRqd8Yidg

Blog : www.seriousearning.blogspot.pt

Thank you

MAX

Useful tips.

- Never give useless content in your book. Always provide something beneficial and useful to your viewers. Think yourself as a buyer of your book and then write and think if I will give this kind of information will I buy it ? Think as if you are the buyer and always write that things which you feel comfortable spending money on.
- Be Focused, never lose hope, stick with it. Don't expect a high income in the starting, it takes time just like any other business. Keep on working and surely you will get fruitful result.
- Give the information in the new book relevant to your previous book, do not change the main theme. Just I have written before also if you are writing about the recipes, keep on writing about that thing only don't start writing on marketing, farming or automobile engineering etc. This way you will not land anywhere.
- Keep on adding new books to your virtual library.
- Give something convincing in the description and in the first 2-3 pages because that will lead your sale.
- Try to give a good title, because something sets up in the subconscious mind of the people just by looking at the title so, it should not give something negative or opposing.
- For public domain books, read it yourself first before publishing it otherwise you will not succeed. If you read you will know the content of the book and from the response you will get an estimate about what kind of content is selling more so you can provide that kind of books only. You will get to know the taste of your audience.

Well at last I would like to congratulate you on reading this book and thank you for your kind support. Stay tuned because a lot is coming to making money from home online. I am going to add a lot of different methods that you can use to make some money sitting at home. I am only going to write about that I myself try and get success in it. Only those methods which do not need any money to make money.

" HAPPY WRITING "

GOD BLESS ALL . . . .

MAX.

YouTube Channel :

https://www.youtube.com/channel/UC17jVFBVBhQWv1FRqd8Yidg

Blog : https://www.seriousearning.blogspot.pt

www.ingramcontent.com/pod-product-compliance
Lightning Source LLC
Chambersburg PA
CBHW081821170526
45167CB00008B/3490